THE BUSH
BECKONS

TORN CURTAIN PUBLISHING
Wellington, New Zealand
www.torncurtainpublishing.com

ISBN Softcover 978-1-991299-02-4
ISBN EPub 978-1-991299-03-1

Typeset in Poppins and Minion Pro

Original cover art by Winendra Adi. Used with permission.

Cataloguing in Publishing Data
  Title: The Bush Beckons
  Author: Linda Watt
  Subjects: Personal memoir, Australian life, Faith-based testimony, Equine care, Abuse and recovery, Spiritual life.

A copy of this title is held at the National Library of New Zealand.

Linda gives us a vivid glimpse into her life and loves with startling clarity and honesty. I taught her at Bible College and admired her quest for truth and wholeness and her compassionate support for so many people. Her journey in life will inspire and encourage you in yours. God's love and grace transformed Linda's life as it can transform yours, and her story can fill you with hope and faith in your own journey through life. You'll be blessed and inspired as you read and will probably pray the same honest, heartfelt prayers typical of Linda.

—Geoff Waugh

Founding editor of the *Renewal Journal,* author of *The Life of Jesus* and over twenty books on ministry and mission

You will find hope in this account of God's love for a woman who is desperately searching for a Savior. You will be inspired as you read this miraculous story of God's ability to pick up the pieces of a broken life and fully restore it for His honour and glory. Linda's unique story shines a light on God's redemptive work of grace and love.

—Kate Dreston

Christian author, podcast host, and founder of Kate Dreston Ministries

This is a deeply personal and radical autobiography of a woman rescued, redeemed, and ultimately completely and irrevocably transformed by the grace of God. With captivating style, Linda shares her loves and lures, trials and triumphs, family and fears. Often confronting and raw in its imagery, this stark and honest account presents the reality that was hers and offers a way forward for readers amid their own struggles. Any who are passionate about embracing life's challenges and opportunities need this book on their shelves. Anyone involved in caring professions will find this a useful resource. I highly recommend it!

—Reverend Dave Thomas
Uniting Church Minister

The Bush Beckons is a fascinating read that tracks the various ages and stages of Linda Watt's incredible journey. Life has required much of Linda, leaving her to navigate times of scarcity, betrayal of trust and seasons of barrenness. She's arrived on the other side of these challenges, not just surviving, but thriving. For anyone dealing with major transitions and needing to discover the hope to start over, this book is for you.

—Jonathon Schroder
Senior Pastor, Axis Church

If you are thirsty for hope, encouragement, or simply the reassurance that lives can turn around and hearts really can be healed, this is a book you won't want to ignore. With good humour and characteristic steadiness, Linda walks her readers down the bush tracks of her life, navigating the bumps, dodging peril, avoiding the ruts, and ultimately making it to a destination where she finds peace and safety. A beautiful account of resilience in the face of hardships and the capacity of kind-hearted people to touch a life in significant, lasting ways, *The Bush Beckons* is a story that will delight, inspire and captivate even the most casual reader.

—Anya McKee
Head of Culture and Quality, Torn Curtain Publishing

THE BUSH BECKONS

An Aussie Woman's Story
of Finding Home

LINDA WATT

For my miracles

CHAPTER ONE

DAD'S REMEDY FOR MY broken heart was a one-way ticket to a country full of strangers.

I wore the skirt and short-sleeved top I'd sewn from light white cotton splattered liberally with sweet blue flowers. It was my first time on a plane, and I felt small as I walked past the other passengers towards the plane's tail-end and stretched on tiptoes to reach the overhead bag storage.

Seventeen. Was that old enough? Old enough to die? I couldn't muster enough pieces of my shattered heart to decide, or to hope that changing countries would make a scrap of difference.

IT WAS POST-WAR, 1952. Italy was slowly rebuilding, scarce on manpower, animals, tools, root-crops, and seeds. One day, a council man visited their small Abruzzi farm to inform my father's family that ten men from the province of Chieti would be selected to emigrate to Australia. It was a once-in-a-lifetime opportunity, and he suggested the youngest brother of two should apply.

At the age of twenty-four, leaving his home country had never crossed my father's mind. But as he thought about it and reasoned with his father, he agreed that if he was accepted (which was unlikely), he would return home within two years. His father, wanting to guarantee the safety—and sure return—of his son, insisted on buying a comprehensive insurance policy. The insurance money would be kept in an Australian bank account, and the family could rest easy knowing funds were available to bring my father home if he got sick or injured overseas. It would also allow him to return in good time to fulfil the arrangement between his family and another—to marry their daughter.

The emigration process was rigorous, and any hint of association with the mafia resulted in instant disqualification. But in what he calls destiny, my father was one of the chosen ten emigrants, and farewelling his Italian *famiglia,* he set sail on the *San Giorgio* bound for the land 'down under'. Perhaps 'destiny' would have docked his ship had he known he would never see his father or stepmother again.

For forty-four days the brave adventurers voyaged across the Indian Ocean. On board, Dad offered free, amateur haircuts which greatly offended the ship's barber—a story he'll happily recount if you have an hour or so to spare. Dad often says, "to make the story short . . ." but it never is—so be prepared to settle in!

When the ship finally disembarked in Melbourne, a group of passengers, including Dad, were taken by train to the Bonegilla Migrant camp set up by the Australian Government to receive and train migrants and refugees. The first and most pressing challenge was to learn English. Speaking the language would help with the second challenge of securing a job.

The arranged marriage back home to a woman he hardly knew, morphed into a plan to wed by proxy with Dad's brother standing in for him in Italy. But those plans quickly faded into the Australian landscape and melted away under the hot outback sun, when Dad met a beautiful, gentle Aussie woman in a small corner store. Fortunately, his betrothed in Italy was relieved as, in Dad's absence, she too had fallen in love with someone else.

Six-and-a-half years after disembarking on its shores, Dad pledged his commitment to Australia. This meant renouncing his Italian citizenship. It would be thirty-six years before he visited Italy again, long after his father and stepmother were gone.

Unlike Dad, my mother had never travelled outside her home country. Mum was born into a family living in a dirt-floor hut on an island off the coast of Queensland, and the kids spent their early childhood gloriously barefooted, bare-chested and bareheaded, swimming in a pristine ocean and climbing rocky cliff sides with ease. The poverty that overshadowed Mum's otherwise idyllic childhood intensified considerably when her father discarded his wife and five children for another woman. Back then, only widows received government assistance payments—not deserted wives—and my grandmother was left with six mouths to feed and no income.

The family survived on pippies, cockles, oysters, the occasional stranded shark, fruit which was plentiful on the island, and bags of offal that came over on the boat once a month. With no fridge, the heart and liver were eaten in the first couple of days, while the tongue and tripe lasted longer. Their greens were pigweed and wild spinach. An industrious woman, Grandma crafted beautiful bark pictures on cards and made souvenirs from shells and sand, which the soldiers bought when they came to the island in the troop ships. Nothing was wasted and every sugar bag and flour sack, every piece of brown paper and string, was a treasure to be repurposed. Clothes were made from calico bags, toilet paper squares were cut from newspapers, and furniture was created out of kerosene tins. When an orange or an apple washed up on the beach from a troop ship, it was cause for great jubilation. Mum found out many years later that her mother also caught the ferry to the mainland once a week to pick up food from the Salvation Army or Red Cross.

Like her mother before her, Mum lived on two sayings, one taken from a poem by Robert Lindsay Gordon: "[In this world of] froth and bubble, two things stand like stone: kindness in another's trouble, courage in your own," and the other from Mother Teresa: "We can do no great things, only small things with great love." A trained midwife, Mum was generous with her gentleness towards every needy creature, human or animal. Neglected neighbourhood women and children often found a home in her heart and at times under our roof. The hand-made cotton frocks Mum wore were often threadbare, but I always thought she looked beautiful, probably because I never heard a swear word or a lie cross her lips.

My newly married parents settled on ten acres of mozzie-infested swamp and bushland in Queensland. Section by section, they laboriously built a house starting with rocks and sand scrounged from roadsides for the foundation. Dad cut timber from trees on local properties, and second-hand nails were straightened out to use them a second time. Mum mixed wheelbarrows full of cement which she lugged to Dad, who slathered it between bricks to build the walls. No power, no running water, few tools—it was a pioneer's life.

While they built the house, they bunked in with a nearby relative whose shack was so small they had to sleep on a mattress laid on a timber door, which in turn was balanced over the top of a bathtub. They moved into the beginnings of their own home when two walls were high enough to lay a sheet of roofing iron across the corner. This primitive shelter was shared with a goat or two and some chooks, plus unwelcome visitors such as snakes—"big, bad, jumping ones," Dad said—and a plague of relentless mosquitoes. The one cow they had was a godsend—not least because of her poo. While working around the farm to clear the ground and plant vegetables, one could tie a tin of smouldering cow manure onto their belts to dissuade the hordes of vampire mozzies.

Small-crop farming was a tough gig. When beans grew bountifully, every farmer had them in great quantities, forcing growers to practically give them away. During a potato glut, the family ate spuds for every meal until even the goat and the dog said enough is enough, and Dad vowed he'd never eat another spud.

"THAT'S NOT A BABY . . . that's a monkey!" Mum had just birthed her second child and first daughter, and I don't imagine Dad's unflattering assessment brought her any comfort in her exhaustion. It didn't bother me though. Like a Spanish Lipizzaner foal—born black to turn white—my dark hair transitioned to glistening blonde before I was toddling. And with the lone camera in our family residing with an uncle at 'whoop whoop'—way out bush—I remained ignorant of Dad's shocked first assessment. Destined to be a horse-lover, I was born on the southern hemisphere's official horses' birthday.

Before diversifying into chicken farming full time, Dad

worked as a fettler on the local railway line. That swung the lead on Mum to do the bulk of the farm work. While she planted and picked strawberries and gherkins, and looked after the growing flock of chickens, she confined me to a cardboard box which she dragged along the ends of the veggie rows. My older brother ate strawberries and knew to stay within 'cooee'.

My job was to scoop fistfuls of sandy dirt into my mouth. And whenever I could grab the juicy, tangy pigweed which grew wild and plentiful, I gleefully munched on that too. As daylight waned, Mum stripped off our fit-for-rags clothes and bathed my brother and me in the outdoor copper tub with a handful of Condy's crystals. Mum hoped it would sterilise the swollen mozzie bites on our arms and legs, that we'd scratched til they were puffy and bleeding.

Ours was a 'less is more' childhood. Aside from having to wear two left boots as soon as I started walking—they still failed in their attempt to straighten my mis-bent left foot—my feet weren't imprisoned until high school. So much easier and safer to climb trees barefoot, and who cared that our feet dried and split in the winter frosts? Not us! Bare feet meant freedom. So did long pants. On that glorious day when Mum finally allowed me to wear them, I pulled up the ugly, ill-fitting, fawn-coloured strides and felt like I'd grown wings to fly.

Unless she was busy having another baby—she ended up having five—Mum was home every day after school with afternoon tea set on the table. The familiarity and care of this routine was always important to me, and on the rare times when she wasn't home, my world suddenly felt out of kilter. On one occasion when Mum was in hospital, Dad fed us stale bread soaked in milk and topped with sugar. It was kind of nice! But I missed the security of knowing Mum would be there at the end of a long school day.

Birthdays meant special treats of soft drinks and cake. Sometimes we had light, sweet pastries called 'puftaloons' stuffed with the cream that Mum had whipped off the top of the fresh cow's milk, and we washed them down with homemade ginger beer. Mum made this delicious drink herself—until the night a cacophony of explosions and banging woke us all up with a fright. All the ginger beer bottles had exploded inside the kitchen cupboard, and after cleaning up that mess, Mum found that her ginger beer-making bug had sadly died.

Christmas took forever to arrive at our place. First came November's Guy Fawkes night, when we took our hard-come-by ha'pennies to the corner store to purchase fireworks—Tom Thumbs, Catherine wheels and sparklers—and gathered at friends' places around backyard bonfires. The bigger, braver kids held 'double bungers' alight in their hands, ignoring parental horror stories of boys and girls who'd had their fingers blown off.

Then, all of a sudden, the Christmas beetles would appear and we knew Christmas itself was a-comin'. Brown beetles hit the doors in droves, begging to be let inside to dance with the lights. Magically, every so often, a wondrous golden-winged one arrived. Their spikey feet gripped our fingers as we admired their shiny backs, before their brown antennas rose up, followed by their glittering wings—and off they'd fly again.

Before the pine tree that Dad cut from the bush was allowed inside the house, we kids had to clean. It was blackmail for sure, but mostly it just meant removing Daddy Long Legs spiderwebs from the corners so that we could hang the green and red crepe-paper chains we'd made. Christmas lunches were feasts—freshly killed, plucked and cooked chickens, roast corncobs, moist plum pudding with hidden shillings inside, and huge slices of sugar-sweet watermelon too loaded with bright red juice to eat indoors. Our Santa stockings were pillowcases, still endowed with a gift even after the heart-breaking revelation that the man in red was a fraud. I can still smell the scent of a brand new plastic doll with 'Kiss Me' written on the bottom of her shoes.

Mum knew our childhood would all too soon be swallowed up in adult responsibilities, so she made sure our carefree days stretched out for as long as possible. We used up every ounce of daylight and found it a great imposition when we had to climb out of gullies and down from our cubby-houses in the trees to come inside and clean up for dinner.

As well as our clothes, the other threadbare item in our house was the ugly, faded grey lino. The holes worn in the main traffic areas grew bigger every time someone walked across them and kicked the edges, chipping off more bits. We tried to avoid the holes, walking around them, and that was pretty much the snuggly code our family lived by—walk around the problems. Avoid conflict. Keep the peace. Don't rock the boat.

The boat for us was Dad's anger. He was the guy who would give you the shirt off his back, but when his volatile Italian fury erupted like Vesuvius, we kids scattered in different directions and didn't come back until he'd cooled off. It was a good thing we had ten acres in which to make ourselves scarce. Dad wouldn't put up with us sitting inside during the day doing nothing, so if he found us idle, we'd be instructed to either get outside or to pick up a broom and sweep the floor. If he was sitting down and we caused any kind of stir, his threat was, "If I get up, I'll murder you!" We were pretty confident he wouldn't get up though, so that one went through to the keeper. However, these early expectations set me on a track of always needing to be active; to keep busy doing something—anything—as long as it wasn't relaxing.

Apart from Dad's anger and the rare medical emergency— like when my youngest brother had febrile fits and Mum panicked—there were few extremes of emotions such as heart-breaking grief or knee-slapping laughter. There was no strategy modelled for dealing with conflict, and early on I knew that what happened inside my heart had to stay inside my heart. Stuff, stuff, stuff things down so you don't lose emotional control.

I know my parents did the best they could to raise us and provide for our many needs. We might not have heard 'I love you', but there was never a doubt in our minds that it was so. Despite the fact that Dad's mother had died when he was six, and Mum's father had abandoned her family when she was seven, our parents did their best to equip us five kids with a steady moral compass. We knew right from wrong and, growing up on the farm, Mum and Dad stuffed our pockets full of childhood memories that money couldn't buy—even *if* there had been money to spare.

Then one day, they gave me the greatest gift of all.

CHAPTER
TWO

ALL THE 'ORDINARY' FLED from my life the moment I saw him. Having walked home from school as usual, I rounded the corner of our long driveway that day to see a perfect white pony backing off a horse float. Unspoken questions bolted around my head. *Whose is this? What's it here for? How long is it staying?* Before any of my thoughts could find voice, Mum beamed at me: "This is Snowball. He's yours."

There wasn't a smidgeon of my thirteen-year-old heart not instantly smitten. Open-mouthed, I scarcely dared to believe it—*mine?!* Dad was never confident with horses, but for a long time I had pestered Mum to work on him, hoping they would grant my wildest dream, and constantly begging: "Please can I have a horse?" I tried to defuse their list of concerns with an emphatic "I promise I'll look after it!" and I devoured every horse book I could get my hands on. When every square inch of my bedroom walls had been plastered with horse pictures carefully pulled from horse magazines, I began sticking my prized pictures to the ceiling instead. But now, standing right here in front of me was the real thing!

A delivery man stood beside the float, having just unloaded his cargo, but he might've been in the nuddy for all I noticed. I only had eyes for the beautiful creature before me. As the man drove away, Mum explained the story. Our dairy cow was notorious for jumping the fence into this man's paddock, and the adults had come up with a creative solution, agreeing to swap our recalcitrant milk supply for this gentle, kind-eyed, 12.2-hand-high gelding who stood waiting for me to love him.

Too impatient to wait for a bridle and saddle, I jumped up onto Snowy's bare back. Never mind that I had never learned to ride. I simply steered him with the halter, bounced around a lot, and fell off until I didn't. How blissful was the day we cantered for the first time! Compared to trotting, it was like sitting in a rocking chair instead of a banged-up old Ute.

Every fine afternoon from that day forward, I raced

home from school, threw off my uniform and pulled on my riding gear. Then I would grab two peanut biscuits—one for Snowy and one for me—and scull a glass of milk, ignoring my parents' futile imploring to "Slow down!" and "Have something to eat first!"

There was no time for any of that. I couldn't wait to ride, and as soon as I got a saddle on him we were off around the neighbourhood until dark, exploring every ridable track. Snowy took me places I would never go on my own, opening my world as we ventured further through forests and bushland. My parents' initial fear about who would look after a horse quickly died. I'd sooner go hungry than eat before I had prepared Snowy's feed. Every evening I filled the house with the sweet smell of boiling barley, heaving the heavy chaff cutter around to chop up lucerne hay, and mixing it with warm bran and water.

I left my school friends to their crazy obsessions about the latest hairstyles, dresses, and makeup. I didn't care two hoots about such trivial things. The smell of Snowy's sweaty neck and his leather gear were perfume from heaven, and I lived in riding gear. It was just as well, as Dad was of the firm opinion that anyone who wore makeup or perfume was almost certainly a prostitute. My one attempt at wearing nail polish had caused as much drama at home as the exploding ginger beer bottles. But nothing mattered to me as much as my wonderful horse.

My father was extremely strict with my older brother and me. Perhaps that's why riding was such a joy—it was the one thing I was allowed to do. Luckily for them, Dad mellowed somewhat after the other kids came along. One happy memory I have of my father was the day he took me to the Children's Hospital in Brisbane to have a boil lanced on my backside. After the lancing we went to see an Elvis Presley movie together. It is the only time I remember Dad and me doing anything special—just the two of us.

Outings with Mum were also rare. Occasionally she and I shared a milkshake in the city, but it was usually just before a visit to the dreaded, white-coated dentist who would thrust a horse-sized syringe into my tender gums and drill for hours on end, eventually filling every molar in my head. With my parents tied to the farm, there was very little time for anything but work.

I could not imagine life without Snowy. His noble, gentle and wordless friendship (if you don't count whinnies) made me feel safe and needed. I was responsible for his health and well-being, and he provided mine. I had never been happier.

Which is why, on that dreadful morning when I found him lying flat on the ground in the stable, drenched in sweat and groaning deeply as he strained to roll over, instant terror filled my heart. My thoughts immediately turned to every horse owner's worst nightmare—colic. Propelled by fear, I raced up the road and across the railway line to beg Mr Storey for help.

Mr Storey was in his sixties, had legs that were permanently bowed like he was on horseback, and never used a word that didn't need saying. Despite this, he had patiently taught me various bush remedies for horse ailments. I visited him often, soaking up his wisdom as I observed the gentle and confident way he handled my horse. Mum reckoned that every time Snowy sneezed, I took him up to see Mr Storey. But that day, as I willed my legs to run faster, dread sank into my gut like a stone. I knew that Snowy was in severe pain, and if colic was the cause, this was deadly serious. If the intestine twisted around itself, cutting off the blood supply, it would be fatal. My heart pounded. Snowy was my responsibility, my teacher, my road to freedom. If I lost him, it felt like I would lose everything. My life would become a big fat zero.

I landed on Mr Storey's doorstep, gasping and sputtering words of emergency. Jumping from foot to foot I tried to be very patient while he gathered a long hose and a large bottle of beer and threw them into his truck, then drove us back down the road I'd just run up. Once we were in the stable, Mr Storey forced Snowy to stand up, lifted my horse's trembling, lead-weight head and carefully eased the hose down one nostril. He fed the hose all the way into Snowy's stomach, then poured the whole bottle of beer down the hose. When he finally pulled the hose out, Mr Storey turned to me with a solemn face. "Walk him," he said. "Don't let him lie down. If he pees, then you know he'll be right."

One painful step at a time, Snowy slowly walked around the paddock with me leading. His head hung low to the ground and his eyes remained semi-closed, but he kept walking. He knew I was trying to help him and he followed, trusting me to lead him through this trial. I alternated between willing with all my might for Snowy to be saved and rubbing his neck to reassure us both. It felt like an eternity passed before he suddenly pulled up, stretched his front legs with a deep groan, and lifted his tail as he peed. Never had I been so thankful to see a horse relieve itself. My heart swelled with joy, and as from that moment Mr Storey was my favourite person in the world!

THE WINNER'S CIRCLE AT our local horse shows typically belonged to young riders whose fathers could afford top-dollar horses, fancy floats, and expensive lessons and gear. Of course, I didn't fit that category, and I didn't bring home handfuls of ribbons—so whenever a judge reached up to shake my hand and tie a prize ribbon around Snowy's neck, my heart would swell, knowing we'd gone the long way round to earn it.

I adored my older brother, but one day before a gymkhana, my adoration threatened to slip a notch. On our property grew a large mulberry tree, prized for its luscious and juicy fruit which Mum transformed into famously delicious pies. I'm unsure as to what wickedness overtook Tony this day. Perhaps it was that all his attempts at horse riding ended in comical failure, as every time he gingerly climbed on Snowy and coaxed him into a walk, Snowy found a tree to walk underneath—one with a branch hovering at just the right height to swipe off an unbalanced passenger.

I had left Snowy in the house yard so he wouldn't traipse down to the dam—where he liked to fill his belly with water lilies—and end up mud-stained before the big day.

Meanwhile, I filled a bucket with warm, soapy water, ready to wash him, bandage his legs, and finally stable him to keep him clean for the next day's event. Humping a bucket of sloshing water, I rounded the corner to find not my grey pony, but a zebra! Huge purple stripes circled Snowy's entire body, and I dropped my bucket in shock, squealing like a stuck pig.

"Mum! Come see what Tony has done!"

People have always told me I don't look Italian—my blonde hair and fair skin belie that half of my heritage. But right then, gaping at my zebra show-pony, my blood ran red-hot Italian. Tony had wisely made himself scarce, so all I could do was wash Snowy one fury-fuelled round after another. I scrubbed and brushed until my arms ached, fighting the stubborn fruit juice that had leeched into Snowy's beautiful coat. Even so, it was a dull, mulberry-stained zebra that I rode in the gymkhana the next day. And I never did get even with Tony.

WE WEREN'T EXACTLY PEAS in a pod, but my best friend Marisa loved horses just as much as I did. In fact, we first met when we were both out riding, discovering—to our delight—that we lived less than a kilometre apart! Like me, she wasn't too interested in being studious at school, and she loved playing basketball. And really, what else mattered? It didn't matter that we were both from Italian stock, which made us 'social misfits', especially at school where Marisa was called a 'Wog' because she was full-blooded Italian, complete with olive skin, dark hair, and a feisty spirit. Still, we didn't take the slights seriously—at school I'd even sometimes sing a song about being a 'half-breed'—it just made us feel we were more special than the average Aussie kid.

Despite Marisa and I quickly becoming best friends, both sets of parents were firmly convinced that the other girl was a bad influence on their own daughter. Thankfully, because our horses were our life, we weren't often in each other's homes. But anytime I happened to be in close proximity, I became the subject of her parents' heated discussions. And, judging by the unmistakable tone, they weren't speaking of me in a good way. I was glad I couldn't understand the language.

Some mornings, I awoke to a soft *tap tap tap* on my bedroom window. It was always Marisa, knocking softly so my parents wouldn't wake up. We had discovered that daylight fled too early after a long school day, so we'd ride out at four-thirty, in the morning's pre-dawn light instead. We'd take to the trails with chatter and laughter and dreams of running away with our horses and riding all around Australia.

On hot Saturday rides we'd strip off our horses' sweat-soaked gear, following suit ourselves down to our togs. Then we'd ride bareback to the dam on our property where she-oaks, scrub wattle and paperbarks stood guard along the banks. Their colourful trunks added a flair of fun to our swimming hole. In fact, there were so many shades and textures that my artistic grandmother loved to create scenic pictures using the fine layers of tea tree bark as her medium.

Marisa and I confidently led our horses right into the dam until the water reached halfway up their bellies. Then, as they gorged contentedly on juicy waterlilies, we'd leap off their backs and land in the water with a heavy splash, squealing and laughing, clambering up our patient mounts and jumping off again and again. We weren't keen to stand on the squelchy, muddy bottom, or to linger too long in the murky water. Too many carnivorous, mucus-covered eels slithered easily through the gloom below. Still, despite their creepy vibes, I had tasted cooked eel once and was surprised to find it wasn't half bad. Far less threatening were the

Billabong mussels scattered around the dam's banks. The hard-shelled molluscs sucked in the cloudy water, only to filter it and spit it back out again. We trekked to our water playground most summer weekends, and by the time we all emerged from the tea tree-stained waters, both horses and riders wore a film of brown slime and needed a good hose-down.

On Sundays, we set out on the seven kilometre trek to the Pony Club, then headed back after a full day's riding. Often, I was so done in that I would give Snowy his head, knowing he'd bring me home on autopilot. I'd hook the reins over the saddle, kick my feet out of the stirrups, and half doze off in the fading light. Even in the dark, my horse knew exactly where his feed was, and he was keen to get there! They were long and exhausting days, but I loved every minute. Years later, when I no longer lived at home and my younger sister began riding, Mum and Dad bought a horse float, and Dad drove her to the pony club. But I reckon she missed out on half the fun!

"They all have to be smoked before we go home."

Marisa and I were riding with another friend who suddenly fished a packet of ten cigarettes out of her sock. It was a good thing the horses walked along steadily that day, because I had to drop both reins to pick out a cigarette and light it. My first drag tasted obnoxious. *Who in their right mind would enjoy this?* Not wanting to feel like a naive outsider, I persisted with my puffing, knowing I probably wasn't doing it right because the other girls' smoke streamed out of their noses like a steam-train stack. But soon enough, I was a thirteen-year-old smoker, hiding my own packets of cigarettes in my socks.

Dad had always told us not to smoke, but since he smoked I didn't take it much to heart. But my brother Tony disapproved of my secret habit. Walking home from school one afternoon, he grabbed my cigarettes and, proceeding in front of me, dropped them on the ground one at a time, a few metres apart. Perhaps I should have interpreted that as him caring about me—like I did for him the time he fell off his bike and skinned the warts off his knee and I found some newspaper and wrapped his knee to stop the bleeding— but I was angry and embarrassed. I felt a bit tramp-like as I stooped to pick up my smokes.

When Snowy retired after a painful hoof disease left him lame, every horse thereafter came with problems. Between strangles (a debilitating respiratory tract disease), one horse who was a bolter, another who reared over backwards, and still another who soon learned he could better my feeble-wristed strength, I wondered if I'd ever find another good horse. Word on the 'horse street' was that if anyone owned a decent horse, they wouldn't sell it. Then along came Soxie—a floppy-eared, big bay gelding. I wished I could call him my own, but the truth is he was on loan. Still, we won some prizes together, and I especially loved the blood-pumping excitement of cross-country jumping. Soxie's powerful strides would swallow up the ground and send our combined weight flying over fallen logs and bush jumps. Despite the floppy ears, he also scrubbed up and performed well in dressage.

My heart and freedom were found on the back of a horse. No one to tell me what I had to do now . . . or next. When I wasn't riding, my imagination was, and my daydreams drove me down a dusty road in a horse-drawn wagon . . .

"You smell!" I laughed and bumped the border collie dog who perched beside me on the wagon seat. His bright eyes

looked around intently as I drove, and I shared his keen
enthusiasm for the day, breathing deeply the eucalyptus smell
and the hint of damp in the air while trying to match bird
calls to their owners in the majestic gums. Thick leather reins
weighed heavy in my hands then ran through the harness to
the horse's bridle. His clip-clop, clip-clop kept beat with the
relaxed rhythm of my heart. Our wagon wheels rattled, leaving
behind rim tracks, our dusty wake, and every responsibility.
The bush called me into its solitude, and I went gladly.

Lengthening shadows meant it was time to make camp.
Unharnessed and hobbled, my horse didn't wander far. The
dog chased shadows and threw himself ecstatically into the
tea-tree-stained waterholes. Good on him for having fun while
I gathered sticks for the fire. The smell of damper baking in
the hot coals was as good as a whistle to call him back. Filling
our bellies on damper dripping with golden syrup, mine was
washed down with black billy tea, boiled over the fire.

I reckon if there's a heaven on earth, this is it. Lying under
an open sky shimmering with stars, my dog and I drift into
fearless sleep to the crescendo of cicadas. At the beginning of
the next day, a family of cackling kookaburras and hordes of
chirruping crickets call in the morning. The bush beckons us
into endless rising dawns and settling dusks, out of earshot

of any motor, and with only safe adventures waiting around
every bend in the dirt track . . .

All too soon the dream would come to a rude end with
the sound of a recess bell or the scolding of a teacher. School
got in the way of my dreams a bit. I still hadn't found a good
use for it, and high school and I got off to a bad start.

CHAPTER THREE

"YOU'RE STEALING, AREN'T YOU?"

Just moments earlier, my eyes had flicked over a copper coin lying on the ground. It was enough to buy a small paper bag of my favourite sweets at the corner store, and my mouth was already watering at the thought of the milky-bar lollies. Picking up the two-cent treasure, I stored it in my locker for safe keeping . . . just when the school principal was making his rounds.

"What are you doing at the lockers?" Not waiting for an answer, he added in undisguised disgust, "Go and wait outside my office for me!"

Seemed all the bees in his bonnet started stinging when he saw me.

Being the first week of high school, I didn't even know

where his office was. I got directions, then climbed the stairs and waited outside. Dumbfounded, I silently rehearsed the locker rule: only access just after and just before classes. I was positive I was within the 'just after' time.

He soon returned, and I cowered under his authority as he wordlessly waved me inside. It only took him seconds to make his opinion clear: I was a thief, loitering at the lockers to see what I could steal. With his judgement and warning lodged firmly in my chest, I walked out. All the honest 'try' I had started out at high school with, died on the vine. I already felt like a runt in a large litter of high schoolers, and I knew my star would never shine as brightly as my older brother's. In one week, two teachers had already remarked what big shoes I had to fill. But to be branded a thief left me nowhere to go. If the head of school thought so little of me, how could I ever rise above it? Then and there, I decided I couldn't.

It's a shame that proverbial penny (or in my case, two-cent piece) didn't drop, to tell me that taking the easy track might not have been worth it. As time went by, I could almost predict every report card: "Linda could do better if she applied herself." It's not that I wasn't smart. Passing subjects required little effort, but I had shackled myself to the principal's opinion of me. The other short straw was that I had no vision for life beyond school. Not a thing fired my imagination. A single conversation with the school guidance officer presented me with a ho-hum smorgasbord of a nursing, teaching, or secretarial career. Too late, I realised that, had I hog-tied all that promising potential and shone my own star, maybe I could have been a veterinarian or at least ventured in a direction I was interested in, like going to an agricultural college, or exploring rural experiences such as governessing, like Mum did. Maybe it's not your life that gets wasted, but your mind. So, typing and shorthand it was.

Not that all was lost at school. Every fine-weathered lunch hour found me on the basketball court. Five feet, two inches isn't an advantageous height for dunking a ball, but weaving, ducking, and intercepting passes were my forte. I was no sprinter either, but I loved long-distance running. One sports day, a good friend and I paced each other neck-and-neck in the 800-metre race. Rounding the last lap, she had a brainwave: "Let's hold hands and cross the finish line together!" I stretched out my hand in agreement. A few metres short of the finish line, the glitter of gold must have mesmerised her. She dropped my hand as though it was a hot branding iron and bolted flat strap, leaving me flabbergasted in second place, and redefining the meaning of friendship.

A boy or three turned my head in high school, especially that one who wasn't embarrassed for me to see his sweat-drenched singlet after he thrashed out a hard game of basketball. We exchanged carefully-etched, one or two-line treasured love notes on school paper. I folded and unfolded mine so often the folds wore into holes. With school an hour away from home by bus, it was rare to meet outside of school hours, so our feelings were expressed through long, shy gazes and smiles, and hands brushing softly against each other in passing.

Then along came Jamie.

Two years older than me, this very smooth, Fonzie-like guy wasn't just any boy. The difference between other boys and Jamie was like looking at a horse poster on my ceiling versus galloping bareback on my own horse through the forest.

How is it that a boy's eyes can single out your heart and seal it with his ownership with just one look? And when he smiles and one side of his lips curls up in sexy cuteness, how can it seem like you and he are the only beings on the planet? That one, skinny high school boy carried enough weight to bag dibs on every thought and feeling, until my heart had opened towards him like a full-bloomed rose. In the blink of an eye, I wrapped my fourteen-year-old heart all the way around this boy.

Jamie and I first met at a youth hall in his street which was beside a Spanish-looking house that I never gave a second look. One night, he guided me to the back of the youth hall. I'm sure I stopped breathing at his tender look. My legs were wobbling like a jellyfish. "Are you an experienced kisser?" he whispered. My lie quickly became obvious when his kiss overwhelmingly took my breath away. Even a jellyfish had more structure than I did at that point in time. After that, as the weeks and months clicked over, I knew I would forever love this wonderful, gentle boy.

My parents, however, were not ready for Jamie. Maybe it was his golden hair which flowed longer than Snowy's mane, or the fact that, when he got his license, his hotted-up red Ute sputtered down our long driveway scaring the chooks into a panic. Whatever it was, when Jamie came to visit, Dad left no doubt about his disdain. He tucked his vermin-exterminating rifle under his arm, stepped outside, and told my boyfriend to never come back or else he'd use it.

That was not how I had hoped the visit would go. Fighting

tears, the disappointment etched deep into my heart, obliterating any hope that Jamie would be welcomed into my family. I told myself it didn't matter what Dad thought. I knew Jamie and I would be together forever, and if Dad couldn't accept that, then he'd miss out on our happy ever after and on cute mini versions of Jamie and me. So Jamie and I continued to see each other on those rare occasions when, unbeknown to Dad, Mum said I could go out.

ONE WEEK OF GRADE eleven was enough to convince me that my usual coasting-through style wouldn't cut it for the senior grades. I dropped out of school and found my dream job at The Horseman's Bookshop in Albion. Mr Greathead owned the shop. Each day as he arrived at work, I watched him with admiration. His body over-filled the driver's seat of his car, which he steered holding a big black knob affixed to the steering wheel. It took a four-point turn for him to manoeuvre from the car to the pavement, where he would balance steadily on two forearm crutches. This exacted a great amount of energy. One painstaking step after another, he shuffled into the office and landed with a great whoosh into his swivelling leather chair. There he stayed for the day, the sweet-smelling smoke from his pipe filtering through the shop and seeping into the pages of the horse books. He was a good boss, generous and kind, and a loving family man.

A new job wasn't the only big change afoot. My two riding mates were moving in together and needed a third to help pay rent. They asked me to move in with them, but I knew I didn't want to.

"Mum, can I move out of home?"

I hoped like hell Mum would say, "Don't be ridiculous, of course you can't. You're only fifteen."

"Yes, you can go."

She couldn't hear my heart shuddering deep with feelings and concerns I couldn't verbalise. I had needed her to say *"No"* so I could go back to my friends and say, "My mean parents said I can't move in with you. Sorry." Nothing in me was ready—or wanted—to leave home, but I was too spineless to say so.

When we moved into the rental house with hardly a lick of furniture, it was no more than a roof over our immature heads. None of us knew how to cook, we didn't like housework, and the cost of renting was a shock!

Overnight, the narrow little bush track of my life had

detoured onto a main highway with not a red light or vermin extinguishing rifle in sight. Now Jamie and I were free to express our love in the way I only ever would for the one man who was my forever.

How could I know it was a highway to hell . . .

"Jamie is in Redcliffe Hospital."

The words pounded in my ears as Marisa drove us the billion miles to the local hospital. All I knew was that he had been in a speed-related car accident and that his best mates—the driver and the front-seat passenger—had both been killed. Jamie had been in the back of the vehicle. I couldn't catch enough breath as I sat forward in the passenger seat willing the car to go faster, to get me to Jamie's side, to find out how badly he was injured. He would need me now more than ever.

I blinked at the young woman perched beside him on the hospital bed.

Who is she? Who is this woman sitting by my love's side, holding his hand and whispering an audible, "Darling" into his ear?

"Maybe she's his cousin," Marisa offered kindly.

Maybe my heart was about to be smashed to smithereens.

Jamie blinked at me through puffy eyes, and suddenly aware they weren't alone, they ended their shared intimacies. She glanced at me without emotion, perhaps confident that she was the winner in a game I'd had no idea was a competition, or perhaps because Jamie lay broken, bloodied and battling the reality that his two closest friends were dead. Whatever her reasons, she said nothing as she rose and walked out of the room. Perhaps Jamie had told her *I* was his cousin.

Saturated with grief and confusion, I willed my feet to move to the bed. That was my place—sitting close to Jamie—but she had stolen it. I stood quietly beside his battered body. Six soft words made their way through his smashed teeth, and they crashed full force into my heart: "That's the way the cookie crumbles."

And just like that damned cookie, my world crumbled . . . crumbled like an unwanted biscuit that a man had held in the palm of his hand and then suddenly crushed, letting it fall all over the floor at his feet. *Why wasn't I chosen? Why wasn't I good enough? What was wrong with me?*

My heart tried to escape the pain by beating its way out

of my chest. Its pulse pounded in my temples. My breath came shallower and shallower like a tide going out and not coming back in. My chest felt trapped in a vice. I knew this wasn't the time to unleash emotions. I knew I must walk around this gaping hole long enough to be strong for Jamie.

Tenderly, I kissed an unmangled spot on his forehead and answered softly, "Don't worry about it. You just get better." Then I walked away. Marisa must have steered me out of the hospital, but it was into a gaping empty world—one that I didn't know how to navigate without Jamie.

Time blurred, but sometime soon after, I moved back to the farm. Knowing my tomorrows wouldn't work without Jamie, two realities cemented their place in my thinking: I had no reason to live. I would need courage to die.

The rose petals had fallen, the fragrance was gone, a heavy gate had been dragged shut and locked, and the key destroyed. The precious things I had offered had been rejected and now lay irretrievable, gasping in pathetic throes of death. No one would ever be allowed to break my heart again. I locked everyone out and kept all the grief padlocked in.

No one in the family seemed to know how to talk about the inner amputation I'd suffered. Lost, alone, desperate for anything on which to hang even a singular hope, I took my pain to a psychiatrist. One hour later I walked out with it still intact. There had been no connection, no empathy, and hardly even any eye contact as the professional 'people helper' scribbled down notes and appeared to be drawing shapes while I tried to unburden my heart. Offering no strategy for a way forward, the only thing he put in my hands to relieve the pain was a drug to stop my broken heart from beating so heavily. Like one of Dad's chooks with its head cut off, I was still moving but my heart was decapitated: Dead.

The overdose of anti-depressants knocked me out for two days. When I came to, my parents told me they'd bought me a one-way ticket to New Zealand. Many years later, Dad told me he offered me the choice between living with his family in Italy or going to New Zealand, but I have zero memory of it. Everything happened so fast, and I was still reeling from the grief and shock.

The man whose name I had tattooed on my heart came to see me before I left.

Jamie said he hoped I'd do okay.

I said I hoped the same for him . . .

CHAPTER FOUR

My boss, Mr Greathead, had contacts in New Zealand, and he soon arranged a live-in job for me on a stud farm in the South Island. Mucking out stables, feeding and grooming horses, and leading them from the stable to pasture was something I could lose myself in without having to face people. I might not have known a soul in New Zealand, but at least I had a job to go to—and a horsey one at that.

Dressed in my thin summer skirt and top, I stepped off the plane at Christchurch airport into minus one degree Celsius—as prepared as ever. A stranger picked me up at the airport to take me to the stud farm, but along the way we stopped at a shop because "You'll need gumboots." (Not to mention a coat).

As long as I could avoid the foul-mouthed boss and the

staff who took pleasure in teaching newbies their place, the beautiful horses were almost enough to lift my spirits during the day. Nights, however, saw me tossing and turning. Even with doubled-up socks, pants and tops, my body refused to get warm. But the real kicker was the night pervert who stalked my window. I only lasted two weeks before I quit. The boss was ropeable and the guilt bit at me when he said, "That's the last time I hire an Australian girl!" I was sorry I'd ruined the potential chances of other girls, until the man's face leering at me through the window came back into focus. Then I decided maybe I just did those other Aussie girls a favour.

The one friend I'd made at the stud farm resigned with me, and she kindly invited me to her parents' home, where her blue budgie entertained us at meal-times by eating off our plates and drinking from our glasses. After a couple of nights' stay, the good-hearted family recommended I apply for work at the Salvation Army Hostel in Christchurch. Homeless, jobless and joyless, I walked into Christchurch and through the doors of the Railton Hotel. I don't remember what I said during my interview with the short, tubby Salvation Army Officer, but I do remember what *he* said: "You're pathetic." Then he gave me a job waitressing, which mercifully included dormitory accommodation.

One day, I came across the daughter of the man who had told me I was pathetic. She was sobbing loudly, wiping away at her tears. Something had obviously upset her badly. As I watched, she started smiling through watery eyes, raised her hands above her head and said, "Hallelujah. Praise the Lord!" I decided then and there that these God-people were weird.

As a kid, I'd been to a backyard Sunday School a few times, but this was disturbingly different. It became bleedingly obvious that these Salvation Army people possessed an inner strength and a source of peace that I knew nothing about. They loved being together, they loved church, and they walked around singing a lot and looking happy—even when it was clear that bad things had happened.

Their motives also seemed unselfish. Even when one cute guy befriended me, I soon realised he wasn't looking for anything physical out of our relationship. However, they did seem to come down a bit tough on their own. After work, a group of us often went to the local pub. When it was discovered that one of the Salvation Army girls was coming with us, she immediately got the sack, even though she never drank with us. I thought that was a bit harsh, especially since she wasn't joining in the drinking as it was against their rules.

As well as observing the Salvation Army people, I watched and wondered about the people who dined at the hostel where I worked . . . the eerily lifeless-looking woman with deeply sad eyes who left her broccoli on the side of the plate because of a worm in it . . . the serious, straight-faced gentleman who didn't react when the poached egg slipped off the plate I set in front of him and landed right in his lap . . . Looking around at some of the clientele, I realised I wasn't alone in my broken-hearted state. Unlike my religious co-workers, it seemed these people had no source from which to dredge up hope—just like me.

I ached empty over Jamie, but the beauties of New Zealand steadily drew me out and about. I spent most weekends exploring stunning places, which made me miss Jamie a little bit less and also a whole lot more. I took walks along the beautiful willow-lined Avon River and enjoyed moped rides to Akaroa and Arthur's Pass with a friend. After a long soak in a thermal pool at Hanmer Springs, I decided to camp the night on a hill there. During the night, an earwig crawled into my ear, ever after leaving me unable to fall asleep unless my hair is covering my ears.

ONE OF MY FELLOW waitresses was a goofy, fun-loving young woman with long, carrot-top curls. We hit it off right away, but Deb's job at the hotel became short-lived after she began taking heroin to battle her inner demons. On a 'high' one night, she said to me, "Come on, let's go into the city and stay up all night!" We weren't rostered on the next day, so I figured, why not? Besides, I was worried about what might happen to her if she was in the city all night by herself.

We wandered aimlessly around Christchurch, the hour getting later and later, until music drew us into a building. We snuck inside and sat at the back to listen. When the band paused, a young man stood up and passionately implored us: "Your life is empty. Meaningless. Only Jesus Christ can fill the emptiness that plagues you."

How did he know my life was empty? Oozing excitement and delight, he continued, "Jesus' love is so strong, so personal, that He died for you." When he invited people to come down the front to respond, some unseen force drew me out of my seat. Deb frantically grabbed my arm to pull me back down, and I was shocked to see tears streaming liberally down her face. "Don't do it!" she said. "I've tried it. It doesn't work."

Neither does your heroin, I thought, *nor the marijuana*

I've tried.

In a weak whisper I said, "I have to. Something is pulling me to go." Leaving my distressed friend in her seat, I walked towards the front of the room and waited for whatever it was that would happen next. I felt tingly with anticipation, but also curious and unsure. Someone came to speak to me, and I listened to words I didn't fully understand. "Will you give your life to Jesus?"

Will I? I think so. I don't know. Did I? When Deb and I walked out, we were both confused and emotionally spent.

Soon after that, sitting on a bench seat in Christchurch, the "Hallelujah. Praise the Lord!" girl tried talking to me about religious stuff. Pulling out a small Bible, she quoted Romans 3:23, "All have sinned and fallen short of the glory of God" and Romans 6:23, "The wages of sin is death but the free gift of God is eternal life in Christ Jesus." I had zero tolerance for her pitch, and said I wasn't interested, before walking away. I told myself I wasn't searching for anything.

But it seemed I couldn't escape the message. In one of the rooms I stayed in, a poster on the wall read: "Enter through the narrow gate. For wide is the gate and broad is the road that leads to destruction, and many enter through it. But small is the gate and narrow the road that leads to life, and only a few find it" (Matthew 7:13-14).

At the bottom of the picture, a wide road was chock-a-block with people heading towards a pit of surging fire. People at the edge were already falling into the pit. Horror gripped their faces as angry tongues of fire slurped up to envelop them. The top of the picture held a very narrow road, with only a few people dotted along it. These people's faces were serene as they walked a narrow track towards a glistening golden city. That picture seeped into my soul, and I couldn't shake the lingering sense of concern it provoked.

THE WORKERS' ACCOMMODATION AT the Railton Hotel was a large building with a row of small bedrooms strung down one side and common areas spread along the other. The second-to-last in the row, my bedroom was close to the road. It was also the only room that had a knob instead of a deadlock.

One night, a movement disturbed my deep sleep. *Surely it's too early for the night watchman to be waking me for my shift?* Then as I drifted awake, a clearer thought suddenly dawned—he never had. Instantly, I awoke in full to see a man sitting on my bed. He leaned over me, his eyes boring into me, and a powerful terror gripped me by the throat. I couldn't move. I couldn't scream. I tried, but no sound came out. I was screaming on the inside, trying to force the noise out of my throat. For an eternity, nothing—then finally, my horror-filled screams broke out to fill the night with alarm. The man reacted immediately, bolting out of my room and into the alley between the rooms and the hostel, where he busted a hole in the chain-wire fence to get away.

My now fully-fledged screams brought one brave girl racing into my room. We looked around to see the intruder had pocketed my small change and cigarettes, but my blood turned cold when I saw one of my t-shirts lying on the bed where he had left it. *Why would he have a t-shirt on hand? Did he plan to smother my screams with it?* There was no other explanation.

I told my boss, but there was never any follow-up, and I didn't think to take it to the authorities myself. From then on, like a mole underground, I did my best to stay out of sight and—I hoped—out of the mind of the man who had leered at me while I slept. Every time I walked outside, if a man gave me a second look, my heart began thumping like a native drum. *Is that him? Does he recognise me?*

As beautiful as New Zealand was, I couldn't wait to leave. My unsettling encounters with various men had convinced me that the waters here were infested, with fins on every horizon. Three months after arriving, the final impetus came when my childhood friend Marisa told me she was getting married, and she wanted me home to be her bridesmaid. I escaped the New Zealand tiger-sharks and fell straight into the open jaws of an Australian crocodile.

CHAPTER FIVE

"You're pregnant."

The flitting pain in my abdomen had intensified to the point where I could no longer ignore it, and following an examination, Mum and Dad's ancient doctor had reached his confident conclusion.

"No, I'm not!" I argued.

Obviously not happy to have his superior medical knowledge refuted, he stuck to his guns. But I repeated firmly, "It's impossible that I'm pregnant!"

After going around in circles to no avail, he dismissed me with a referral to a gynaecologist who I'm positive he believed would confirm a pregnancy diagnosis.

The gynaecologist was a kind man whose manner reassured me that I was in competent hands. After the examination he said, "You're not pregnant; something else is going on. I'm booking you in for surgery next week so we can have a look." He didn't say what he expected to find, and as I signed the paperwork, I didn't ask.

One minute I was on the operating table, conscious of counting backwards from ten to one (and not getting far), and the next minute I was heaving out my stitched-up guts post-surgery. Lying in the same hospital where Jamie had recovered after his accident, I had no inkling I was about to come face to face with the legacy of his unfaithfulness.

I was grateful when the gynaecologist stood at my bedside and rested his fatherly hand on my shoulder, steadying me for what came next: "I've removed one of your fallopian tubes because it was too far damaged with infection. The other I've cleaned out, but there is still a dormant infection with only a thirty percent chance of recovery. If the antibiotics clear it up, you'll have fifty percent chance of having children. If not, you will be left barren."

My anaesthesia-fogged mind tried to piece together what I'd just heard. A vile infection had been eating away at my fallopian tubes, and now I only had half of one fallopian tube left. I was missing part of my reproductive system, and what was left might not recover.

A deep sense of loss sucked the breath from me, but not a soul counted my tears. Something precious had been ripped from me—not earthly treasures like money or sentimental keepsakes, but something deeply priceless. Something that, once gone, could never be replaced. Jamie had taken my heart. Now it seemed he had also taken my ability to give birth to children.

Locked up behind a heavy, keyless gate, my shattered heart and crumbled dreams lay in pieces. Outside the gate, a further flood had just been hurled across my future, drowning any lingering remnant of hope.

Everything in me was either dead or dying.

"Secretary and driver required for Real Estate Agent," read the local newspaper ad. "Must be available for after-hours and weekend work."

I turned out to be the successful job applicant, although at the interview I learned a driver was needed because the agent had lost his licence due to drink-driving.

In the beginning I enjoyed learning about the real estate business. My job involved meeting clients and accompanying my boss to various house inspections. It also included receipting deposits and typing up sale contracts, and my deadened soul slipped into the distraction of work.

The frequent business trips and after-hours work didn't bother me. I had nowhere else to be. Hour after hour, my boss and I strategised, planned and talked as we drove between appointments or headed out of town for conferences. Over time, the quick-stop takeaway meals evolved into more formal dinners, then to expensive candlelit meals topped off with Cognac. The conversation followed suit, becoming less business focused and more personal. My boss soon made it clear that things weren't all business for him, and somewhere along the way he started to fill the deep vacuum in my heart, and my feelings for him grew.

But I was scared. I knew this was wrong. Ten years my senior, he had a wife and two children—until he didn't want them anymore because of me. He told his family to move out, but before his wife and children left, I met them in person. That's when I saw for myself the devastation of those whose husband and father I had stolen. I had become 'the other woman', the one who stole another woman's place.

Caught up in a tide of longing mixed with well-suppressed shame, I moved into his Spanish-looking house—ironically, the same house I had noticed next door to the youth hall where I first met Jamie. I had no strength to swim out of the slipstream that had become just another part of my flooded, hopeless future.

IF THE WIND BLEW no more than fifteen knots, we motored across Moreton Bay every second weekend to Moreton Island. The island's beauties aren't shy, with long, white beaches, sparkling crystal-clear water, lush greenery, and, where we put our sixteen-foot tinny ashore, not another person in sight. On our trips there and back, I loved sitting on the bow of the boat, gulping in the fresh air and feeling the cool sea spray hitting my face. I perched there even when the waters were rough; otherwise the motor fumes and the swaying motion further back made me feel sick.

In the dreamy solitude of the island we sizzled freshly caught, mouth-watering fish, and camped in sleeping bags right on the sand. I didn't go out to join in the fishing, nor did I swim very far—my wild imagination had every shark in the ocean making a beeline to devour me. Instead, my days were filled with walks and exploring. I loved the isolation—until it meant a four-mile hike to Tangalooma to restock cigarettes.

Early in our relationship, my boss had purchased brightly coloured exotic silk materials and employed a seamstress to make formal dresses for me. He told me he wanted me to enter a beauty contest, and although I started shaking just thinking about parading in front of people and answering questions in public, I went ahead at his insistence.

On the night of the big contest, wearing one of the dresses he'd had made, I placed in the top three. It was then that I allowed myself to wonder: *Was I just a trophy that he wanted to show off?* He was always concerned about the possibility of me gaining weight, and if I put anything sweet to my lips he expressed his disapproval in no uncertain terms. I was relieved when the debacle was over, although I was too insecure to say so.

After a while of working together, the real estate business seemed to be doing well, so we took a holiday to New Zealand. Despite my marred memories of the place, this time I was heading back as a tourist—and I wasn't alone. We hired a car and took to the road to explore both islands, visiting magnificent sights of natural beauty. I especially loved visiting the Franz Josef glacier—even after a huge boulder broke loose and bounced down the ice, missing my head by a fraction.

But the holiday soon turned sour. My boss had booked a motel for three nights, but he only intended to stay for two. Then his plan was for us to quietly slip away in the early hours of the morning without paying. This happened a few times, until booking accommodation became tricky and he began to suspect that motels were ringing ahead to warn other places about the swindling couple possibly headed their way. He had more than enough money to pay, so maybe it was the thrill of getting away with it that he enjoyed. More and more, I was learning that he found excitement in aberrations.

THE ABERRATIONS HEATED UP in the second year of our relationship. That's when I learned that the crack of a man's hand across my face could cause me to urinate involuntarily. I learned that those same hands could hypnotise me, then stick needles into me to prove I wouldn't feel anything while under hypnosis. And I learned that hands that work Ouija boards and all manner of weird, could also induce out-of-body experiences. Lying asleep beside him one night, I was woken by the bed vibrating strongly. His body was lying in the bed next to me, but at the same time I could see the form of his body rising up off the bed.

If you open a curtain in the daylight, it lets the sunlight in. But open a curtain on a pitch-black night and it lets the darkness in. And I was deeply afraid of the darkness I'd let in.

I'd destroyed a family. Marriage was not on the cards for me, as the man I lived with was already married and had no interest in marrying again. My monthly periods had stopped, despite my youth, so I knew the doctor's worst-case scenario had come true, and I would never be able to have children. I felt as ugly and barren as the label I now wore—*de facto*.

Apparently, one can be only nineteen years old, yet feel a century at least. Because those hands that once caressed you, slippery as eels in a dam, have dragged you long and hard through mud and mire and stinking swamp . . .

One day, my boss dragged a stool under the manhole in the hallway ceiling, reached up and slid the cover aside, then crawled up into the roof cavity. He'd seen two men getting out of a car parked in the driveway, and he hissed at me, "Take the chair away," before sliding the cover shut. Trembling, I removed the evidence of his hiding place and did my best to remain calm.

But I couldn't still my shaking hands as I opened the door to a forceful knock. Two official men dressed in suits and serious faces stepped up the cheap excuse for stairs and stated their business: "We're Fraud Squad detectives, Miss, here to see_____. Is he in?"

"N-no. No," I lied.

After verifying I was his secretary, the two exchanged a quick glance then turned back to me. "We'll have to ask you to come with us to police headquarters for questioning. Go and get whatever you need."

Fear washed down my back, making it hard to fetch my bag and key and to close the door behind me. *Lock the door to back up my lie that he isn't home.* Sitting in the back seat of the silver, coffin-like car, I wondered how long he would stay stashed away in the ceiling.

MANY PEOPLE WHO BOUGHT houses through the real estate company, did not have the required ten percent deposit. I was therefore often asked to fudge the contracts to make it look like they did. My best guess, as we drove towards the police station, was that some of our clients whose contracts had fallen through, had reported my boss to powers that be.

At their headquarters, the detectives directed me into a small room, seating me at the interrogation table. Their first words were, "You're his accomplice. We suggest you cooperate and tell us what we want to know, otherwise you could be facing jail time too."

The last line sank into the pit of my stomach. I felt like the table and chair were growing, and I was shrinking into less and less of a somebody. For more than two hours, my legs trembled under that table. One detective badgered me with questions about clients and contracts, while the other recorded my answers. I didn't know what was going to happen to me, but I knew I'd stuffed up good and proper. My life was over. My reputation lay in ruins. I felt trapped and worthless and terrified I might end up in jail.

I had never wanted to be on the wrong side of the law, but as the detectives drove me home afterwards, I sat in the back seat feeling every bit a criminal. When the car finally pulled into the driveway, the older of the two men turned to speak to me: "When you're ready, you pack your bags and give me a call. I'll take you wherever you want to go."

His words were a light that pierced through the black cloud

of my life. *I can get out? I have a choice?* Never before had that possibility entered my thinking. I had always believed my only option was to lay down and die in the dark hole hewn by my own hand. The kind detective's words were a seed that sprouted into the realisation that maybe I could escape. Maybe I could leave.

Soon after the detectives' visit, the court informed me that, as a de facto, I could 'claim privilege' and would therefore not be required to give evidence at the trial. Even so, in the days leading up to the court case, fear almost buried me, but not because I was worried about how it might turn out. It was because the day of the trial was the day I planned to escape.

The day finally came, and I watched my boss' taxi disappear down the driveway.

Frantically, I scooped up my few belongings. The vice on my chest screwed down tighter than ever, as my mind conjured up worst-case scenarios: *Trial postponed . . . Enemy coming back . . . He's coming, he's coming, run, run, RUN . . .*

It only took moments to gather up my things. Then, standing in front of the telephone, I stared down at it, frozen between my fears. Finally, I willed myself to pick up the handpiece and dial. *It's only eight numbers. Take it one at a time. Concentrate. You can do it. One at a time. Just . . .*

make . . . the . . . call . . .

Then I dialled the number.

"I've had enough. Please come and get me."

Get out of the house . . . wait on the road . . . go, go, hurry, hurry . . .

It was the empty shell of my body that crawled into Dad's car. Despite all the hurt and disappointment I'd caused my parents, they had never shut their hearts or their home to me. Their relief was as palpable as mine as they drove me north to the forestry house in Imbil where my brother lived.

I knew the boss wouldn't find me there . . .

CHAPTER SIX

As I SLEPT, MY dreams gave me a leg-up onto a beautiful, golden palomino. Her unshod hooves pounded across the wide-open range as we chased wild cattle and herded them back to timber yards that had seen a century of suns. My lion-hearted horse and I belonged to each other, and only in this wild country could my heart gallop free.

Waking up in a small forestry hut in Imbil, reality slammed me broadside and wrapped around my throat, choking me. Eyes squeezed tightly shut, I willed the heavenly visions back, but they'd vanished. All that remained was a heavy certainty that there was so much in my life I couldn't ride away from on a beautiful palomino horse.

After two weeks hiding in the hut, I was driven back to the family farm by my older brother.

Time trickled away but it didn't matter because I was exactly no-one going exactly nowhere. With blank indifference I filled out various forms applying to the Air Force to be a police officer. I was not tall enough for the civilian police, but being short didn't disqualify me from being in the armed forces. I passed the interview and psych tests, and within a month I received notification that my application was successful. The police force had no vacancies at the time, so instead I was offered training in air traffic control.

LIKE A DOG WITH hunger pains, scratching to get under a chicken-pen fence, a desperate emptiness clawed at my insides. But unlike hunger pains, nothing satisfied the black, gaping hole in me that begged to be filled. If there wasn't more to life than what I had experienced (or knew I could if I had more money), then life wasn't worth it. It was a rip-off. I started thinking of ending this lone, miserable life for good.

With no taste for life but too scared to die, I drifted, lost in no-man's land, until the day my younger brother brought a flyer home from high school inviting young people in the area to a local meeting. For some reason my attention kept boomeranging back to the slip of paper. Knowing my brother wasn't interested, I took the flyer and immediately began an internal fight about whether or not to go. A shy, insecure, pack-a-day smoker, nothing in me was comfortable with joining a group of strangers, but the irresistible pull to attend was unnerving. That Friday night, in the blue Kingswood Holden sedan my parents had gifted me, I drove myself to the private home where this local youth group met.

My thumping heart seemed louder than my tentative knock, which was greeted with a warm welcome. Once inside, I pointed my eyes to the floor and made for a vacant spot on a lounge. I was an observer—watching a dozen young people playing games, chasing and dodging each other and filling the room with squeals and laughter. They weren't trying to jump into bed with each other. These guys and girls were simply friends having fun. They were about my age, but watching them, I felt a hundred years old. They acted so lightly, while I carried the weight of a busted lifetime on my shoulders.

Then the games part of the night ended, and the youth gathered around in a circle, seating themselves on the floor with ease. A lanky young guy strummed a guitar, and

God-songs were sung. Someone handed me an open Bible, and a lesson began. After the discussion, the leader, Jeff, prayed a prayer, and I watched as people started to leave. I hadn't said a word all night. I was an outsider looking in, my headspace blanketed with confusion. I didn't understand what was happening around me or within me. A civil war raged inside between the 'protect myself at all costs' part of me and the part of me that was beating like a drum closer and louder, urging me to find answers I didn't have the questions for.

What was happening to me? My heart felt split open, totally exposed and up against a wall, facing a firing squad of truth against which I had no defence. No one had to tell me that I was one of the crowd of people I had seen on the poster back in New Zealand—a doomed group walking towards a grotesque pit of fire. I didn't know God, but I knew with every inch of my heart that if I died, I would go to hell, guilty to damnation.

Jeff's perceptive eyes were sparkling as he gently asked if I wanted to talk. My burden of guilt was grinding me into the ground, so yes—I wanted to talk. It sounds cleaner to say a volcano erupted than a boil burst, but for me it was more like the boil. The pus of sin and sorrow oozed out as I spilled my story, ending by saying, "It's too late for me. Too much water's gone under the bridge." But the spark in Jeff's eyes never dimmed. I could feel the love and compassion flowing out of him as he spoke into my weak heart: "No—It's never too late! That's what the gospel is all about. Jesus died on the cross for *you*. He paid for your sins, so forgiveness is a free gift! All you have to do is ask Him to forgive you and to come into your life, and He will!"

But could I accept this wondrous gift? I had gone through the motions two years ago in New Zealand, but nothing had changed. In fact, my life had only gotten worse, the black hole growing bigger. But now my heart felt like it was open wide—and I had nowhere else to go. I took a shaky breath.

"Yes, I am willing."

Utterly blank about what to do next, I was relieved when the youth leader helped me talk to God. He prayed, and I repeated his words in a whisper: "Dear Jesus, I give my broken life to You. I am so sorry for all the wrong I have done and for all the right I should have done but didn't. I don't deserve your grace, but please forgive me. I believe in You. I believe You died on the cross to pay for my sins. I accept Your free gift of forgiveness. I want to live for You. Thank You, Jesus. Amen."

In a blink, the heavy load was lifted off my shoulders as Jesus took it onto His. A smile pushed up from deep inside me, and I could feel the light shining in my own eyes now! I had never experienced this level of inner peace before. It filled the place where, just seconds earlier, worry, guilt and shame had been squeezing their long, dark fingers around my throat. *Was this newfound freedom the source of the joy I had witnessed in those other young people?* Then and there, I knew Jesus had truly forgiven my sin and wiped my heart clean. He had given me a second life, and in that moment, I was reborn.

That night, Jesus robbed a grave—mine. He exhumed me from my self-excavated tomb of darkness, calling me out of it and into a light where, for the first time ever, life made sense. I could see it now—a reason to live and a reason to die. Living meant living for Jesus. Dying meant going to be with Him in heaven. John Newton's famous words perfectly expressed what I was experiencing: "Amazing grace, how sweet the sound, that saved a wretch like me. I once was lost but now I'm found, was blind but now I see."

From that night on, I carried a song of great joy in my heart. The change in me was so dramatic that my parents became worried. Was I losing my mind? Had I joined a cult?

Clearly I was going overboard with this God stuff. Mum suggested I see a psychiatrist, and my sister just wanted me out of our shared bedroom! I drove her up the wall playing Evie Tornquist's gospel songs at top volume. Instead of seeing the light glowing in me and coming along to find out more, she just got mad. Even so, nothing could dampen my spirits which had been lifted so miraculously.

In those days, Marisa and her husband were attending a local church, so it seemed a good plan to join them there. I was a starving woman who had discovered the only food source, and I eagerly drove to church twice each Sunday, not caring that this meant two hours of driving. My hunger for God was insatiable, and the sermons I heard in that church hit the bullseye, speaking straight to whatever issue I was facing in my life at the time.

When I was saved, in a straight-out miracle, God instantaneously took away my desire to smoke. A seven-year addiction was broken, just like that. I still battled now and then with the temptation to light up, but it really hit home that I'd be throwing God's gift of freedom back in His face. It also helped that when I said to my youth leader, "You don't mind if I smoke do you?" he immediately replied, "Yes. I do!" Jeff led me through a Bible study for new Christians, and I soon learned that, even though I belonged to Jesus now, a civil war was still going on inside me. It was God's will versus my old desires—and I had to fight to choose obeying God over the rest.

Then, for the second time in my life, another unmissable, inaudible *'Linda, you have to go to this'* opportunity grabbed hold of me during a youth group meeting. The event advertised was a 'Weekend of Witness,' and it would involve a group of students from a local Bible College visiting the church and sharing about how Jesus had changed their lives.

At this point, I wasn't really weighing up decisions like 'to go or not to go'—I was simply following a path that, to me, seemed brightly illuminated. This 'Jesus road' might be narrow, but I was ecstatic to leave that other, broad yet pitch-black, path behind me. Just as the Bible said, the 'Sunrise from on high' had visited me and shone on me as I sat in darkness and the shadow of death, guiding my feet into the way of peace (Luke 1:78-79).

I went along to the Weekend of Witness, listening hungrily as the students spoke enthusiastically about how God was working in their lives. They distributed chunks of clay and asked everyone to mould something representing where they were in their commitment to God. Mine was a very amateurly-shaped figure of me kneeling in surrender to God—whatever or wherever that would mean. I was one hundred percent all in for Him.

As we sat holding our clay works, the college principal stepped to the podium and began to talk about the courses his college offered. With that, a fire was lit inside me. As soon as the service ended, I made a beeline for the principal, almost at a run! I had to find out more about going to Bible College.

Sitting at home were my acceptance papers for employment with the Air Force, and I felt a puff of pride at the no-small-feat of passing the stringent testing of their applicants. But now I stood at a crossroads. If I took the Air Force route, a whole package awaited—the promise of an exciting career complete with financial provision for housing, medical, vacation and retirement needs. None of that was on the table if I took the Bible College path. Familiar as I was with the donkey and the carrot, it only took a milli-second to decide. I stood face-to-face with an opportunity to know Jesus better, and I was ready to leave everything to follow Him.

All was sounding promising as the principal spoke to me about the two-year Diploma of Christian Ministry and the on-site accommodation on the banks of the Brisbane River. But when he mentioned the cost—*two thousand dollars!*—disappointment levelled me. "I can't afford to come," I said. I didn't have a brass razoo, let alone a number with a few zeros after it.

I hadn't yet managed to get my head all the way around believing in something I couldn't see, so the principal's response surprised me. "Don't worry about the money," he said. "If God wants you at college, He will provide the finances." Instantly, hope rekindled. It made sense that if it was God's will for me to go to college, He would make it possible—wouldn't He? Somehow?

It was late 1979 when I told my youth leader, Jeff, that God was calling me to go to Bible College. Soon after my announcement, he and his wife, Jenny, invited me over to share some news of their own—they wanted to pay for half of my fees. To make up the other half, they suggested I find work that fit around my college studies. I was speechless. Since high school, I'd been tossed to and fro and carried about by any wind that blew. But now, for the first time in my life, a clear path stretched out ahead of me. College must be God's plan. He was making it possible! In three months I would be a Bible College resident and student. I could hardly wait.

I felt strangely flat during those three months of waiting, but a source of encouragement came from two close friends of mine who had also become Christians. One, as soon as he met Jesus, went cold turkey off drugs—a miracle in itself—and God even healed his drug-damaged brain! Jesus' love, peace and joy bubbled out of him like an endless spring, and knowing that he needed it more than me, I gave him my Holden Kingswood. It seemed like the kind of thing Jesus would do.

CHAPTER SEVEN

MY GUT WAS AS tight as a rusted-on bolt, but 'mandatory' sealed the deal—I couldn't evade the one-on-one meeting with Rev Colin Warren. The college principal would probe my past and, upon learning I was a marriage breaker, he would think a mountain less of me. No doubt he'd regret encouraging me to come to college and would send me packing. I'd heard "Your sins have been forgiven" quite a bit by now, but my new 'no condemnation' status just didn't feel real for me—especially when not-so-distant memories knocked regular and loud.

Our principal took his fit and wiry body everywhere with determined steps, purpose-driven. One goal. One love. The same love I wanted to pursue. His smile ushered me into his book-lined office, even as I thought to myself, *That smile will be short-lived.* He invited me to take a seat, pulling up a similar chair for himself. As he prayed a blessing over our meeting, I got the impression he had all the time in the world for me. His kindness encouraged my openness as I began to talk about my past, explaining how I came to know Jesus. I kept my head lowered as I spoke, and when I finally dared to glance up at him, I fully expected to see disdain across his face.

I was blown away by the love and acceptance that shone through his eyes instead. As our meeting ended, he gave me a spoken gift: "I believe God has great things in store for you." He prayed for me again, and I walked away from the meeting bewildered. A very different school, a very different principal . . . This time I deserved a guilty verdict, but instead I had received pardon. *Who was this God I was following? Before, He point blank showed me I was heading for hell because of my sins, but now He wanted to get it through to me that my ledger was wiped clean.*

The next day, as I walked along the college path, I looked up to see Rev. Col walking towards me. My head automatically lowered. *Now that he's had time to think about it, he'll realise he's backed a rotten apple.* He stopped alongside me, and my head inched up until my eyes held his gaze. In that wordless greeting, God's love became real to me. Col's eyes overflowed with only love—love from God. Despite everything I'd broken, destroyed, spoiled and wasted, *God loved me*! It *was* real. There was a love so long, so wide, so high and deep that, lining them up, human love was half a droplet in the ocean. Jesus had crossed the chasm to find me, and not the other way around . . . it was a true love story.

After this, nothing would shift the centre of my affection. All my eggs were in the 'loving God basket'. Where Jamie, my boss, and even family 'friends' whose eyes and smiles swam in veiled vile, had cheated and abused me, I knew God never would. I'd found a love that wouldn't be snatched back if I fell on my face. I'd found a Father who cared about broken bodies, shattered hearts, empty lives. I now trusted the only One who didn't depend on anyone else and who wasn't going to turn to ashes and dissolve around me. And as I studied the divinely inspired scriptures, I found truth that was never going to change.

Everything that had previously floated around in my thinking with no place to land, suddenly settled on a firm foundation. It made sense that such a complex universe was created by someone with infinite intelligence. It brought significance to my days, knowing life was not just something to be consumed until death but that I could actually utilise my life by serving God and helping others. After twenty years of lostness, the puzzle pieces finally came together. God made sense of everything for me, and I wondered how people without faith found reasons to keep living in an otherwise meaningless world. I knew now that I couldn't.

I FELT A LITTLE nun-like with my sparse belongings in my small, upstairs room. But I was at college for one thing only—to learn more about Jesus—and I didn't need fancy for that. Education wasn't limited to Christian studies in our communal living. Our rosters included cleaning common rooms, washing dishes, and cleaning the dining room after meals. It all helped to keep the rental costs down.

One morning, I came across the principal on his knees, working to unblock the old toilet system. I couldn't have been more flabbergasted if I'd been watching the Queen sweep her own parlour! *What was the principal doing, down on his knees with his hands in the stinky septic system?* That was the day I understood that good leadership wears work boots and is the last to take them off at day's end. After that, being asked to paint the dorms or do maintenance around the college was no hardship—in fact, it seemed to be a privilege.

Much to my distress, our personal growth included learning to speak in public. When my turn came to share my testimony during the chapel service, fear just about undid me. Trembling and crying, I begged to be excused. "I can't do it! I just can't!" Col wouldn't budge however, and neither his fatherly hand on my shoulder nor his gently insistent, "Yes, you can," reassured me in the slightest. This 'torture' was merely preparation for 'Weekends of Witness'—the same local church event that had introduced me to college. Every fibre within my being trembled as I held the podium in a death grip, plastering my eyes onto my typed notes. But somehow, I got through that first dreaded experience and survived to tell my tale many more times.

Our college lecturers were 'on fire' for Jesus. Often, we students were moved to tears or stayed around after lectures asking for prayer—simply because we had been challenged, convicted of sin, or received a revelation that set us free from burdens we'd been carrying. This was no mere 'mind learning'. The Word of God was truly alive and active in our hearts. The more I grew in knowing Jesus, the more deeply I fell in love with His beauty and wonder. There was nothing weak about Him—He loved fiercely, never withdrew His kindness from the humble, grieved with the broken, and was non-negotiable on sin. A little more of His character unfolded for me each day, and as it did, I knew without a doubt that, within the confines of mortality, no one would ever reach the end of getting to know Him.

Most students worshipped together at the Kangaroo Point Uniting Church, just a stone's throw from the college. As we stood to praise God in song, His power bolted me to the floor. I stood on holy ground and yet I felt so unholy in His presence. But I couldn't have walked out even if I wanted to. I was held in place, bathing in a cleanness so pure that everything else in comparison was a filthy black.

CHAPTER EIGHT

HE SAT AT THE end of one of the long trestle tables, strumming chords on an old guitar covered in Jesus stickers and singing out his love for Jesus. For three days running, every time I glanced over at the far side of the dining room, I noticed the handsome young man noticing me. I shyly watched him play, hiding my smile when, finishing up one song with particular enthusiasm, he lifted his guitar, jumped onto the next table, and slid across the top of it. It seemed he couldn't contain his faith and exuberance.

On the fourth day, our eyes locked across the dining room and my heart betrayed me with a flutter. *Listen up, heart. We've walked this mile before.* I had decided that everything was now out of bounds for my heart, except Jesus. I was in love with Him—so what the heck was my heart doing? *This is where you get sandblasted to oblivion, remember? This is where you get chewed up and spat out in a zillion pieces.* Totally disgruntled, that night I instructed God in no uncertain terms, "If this is the guy You want me to marry, then give me a clear sign. If not, You can just take these feelings away, because I'm not interested!"

The next morning, I was headed for breakfast when the same easy-on-the-eye, blonde, guitar-playing youth worker approached me. He smiled broadly. "We haven't had a chance to talk. How 'bout after lectures we go for a walk?" He had to wait for a response from me, and I wondered if he saw the uncertainty flick through my eyes. *Is this God's way of answering my prayer? Is He giving me the green light to start a friendship?* My emotions jumbled together, but figuring it wasn't a definite 'no' from God, I agreed to meet him later.

As we walked around the block that afternoon, I told him everything—including the improbability of me ever having children. I half hoped it would frighten him out of any interest. But when I got to the part where God removed my nicotine addiction overnight, his excitement was uncontainable. Picking me up, he spun me around, celebrating all that God had done for me, and I was speechless as a clear crack appeared in the walls I'd so firmly constructed around my heart.

Iain and I were opposites. My assignments were handed in days early, while his landed just before midnight on the due date—usually after I had typed them out for him. I was used to carrying the world; he was happy-go-lucky. I was happiest solo; he thrived in groups and was often the centre of the action. One day, I walked out of a function into a group of six of his ex-girlfriends—all very lovely people!

Iain and I had met in week one of college, and after our maiden walk we hung out whenever we could. We spent most evenings sitting on the grass in front of the main buildings, talking until ten o'clock curfew when I had to go inside and upstairs. Finding yourself on the wrong side of the locked door meant needing to come up with a good reason for the night supervisor to be dragged out of bed to let you in.

One cool evening as Iain and I sat talking, Col strode past. I got a shock when, in response to our "Hello" he blasted us in anger: "What are you doing out after curfew? I'm disappointed with you both!" Looking at me, he commanded, "Get to your dorm, now!" We obediently scurried off the lawn and bolted in different directions. Running upstairs, I found the main door to my dorms still wide open. I checked my watch . . . 9.25 p.m. *That's weird!* I checked the alarm clock in my room—same time. *Oh, what?! Col was wrong?!* As a new Christian, starstruck with the man who had quickly become like a spiritual father to me, I'd naively believed that a man that wise and knowing couldn't make a mistake. It was another lesson for me: Inside those work boots, leaders too have feet of clay.

The next morning, Col approached us sheepishly. He explained that yesterday he'd returned from the neighbouring state of New South Wales and had forgotten to adjust his watch back to Queensland time. With a twinkle in his eyes and a grin spread wide across his face, he apologised, then said, "I'll forgive you!"

The second week of college found us at the compulsory orientation camp. During a break in the day's activities, Iain and I went for a walk along the beach. It didn't take him verbalising it for me to know he wanted our relationship to be deeper. But he hadn't said anything outright, so it's no wonder his face paled as if I'd dunked him in the cold surf when, out of the blue, I stopped walking, turned to look him in the eye and said, "If you aren't interested in marrying me—not now, but sometime in the future—then turn and walk away right now. Because I'm not interested in fooling around or getting hurt again." He looked at me soberly. "I've never had anyone say that to me before!"

Not long after arriving back from camp, we packed sausage meat and bread from the college kitchen and carried our picnic lunch across the road to Kangaroo Point cliffs. The steep crags were popular with rock climbers, but I took no notice of their natural beauty as, there between the rocks, Iain went down on one knee and asked me to be his wife. Only six weeks had passed since he had spun me around in that celebratory circle.

IAIN'S FAMILY WERE UNHAPPY about our engagement.

"You have no money."

"You've only just met."

"You should wait until you've both finished your studies."

And with Iain being the youngest of three boys, his mum said what most mums say: "You're my baby, and she's taking you away from me!"

Iain and his two older brothers had been born in Fiji, where his dad worked in the sugar mills. Each son was sent to boarding college in Brisbane, and Iain's turn came when he was ten years old. After that, his parents moved to Australia and settled in North Queensland, where his dad was chief engineer at a local sugar mill. His mum was a seamstress by trade. She made pottery, porcelain and cloth dolls, teddy bears, copper work, jewellery, and upholstery. She also did glass decorating, painted, and played a keyboard. There was little she couldn't put her hand to, and she shared her skills and creations generously in the community.

Iain's parents were right about us having no money. At his father's insistence, Iain had finished his Fitter & Turner qualification before going off to Bible College, but he had no savings. My part-time work vacuuming the psychedelic carpet in a Returned Services League Club (as well as cleaning their windows) and a second job ironing, barely covered the other half of my college fees. Still, we were determined to make it work. The simple yet elegant engagement ring we chose cost two hundred dollars, and we each moved cupboards around in our rooms, looking behind and under them, for coins to help meet the cost.

Shortly after our engagement, Iain told me he believed God was calling him to switch from youth work to training for ordained ministry. He felt he could help people more effectively by working with whole families, not just with the struggling youth. This new dynamic to our future sent my head spinning. It felt like God had lured me into something I *might* be able to handle—being married to a youth worker— only to throw me in the deep end by switching Iain's career choice to a church reverend. *Doesn't God know I'm the absolute least suitable person to be a minister's wife?* I sure did. *Is love going to be enough to get us through this?*

Unlike any other relationship I'd previously been in, both parties loved Jesus and we knew God was drawing us together. Based on that, I felt semi-confident that God knew what He was doing . . . surely?!

JUST BEFORE OUR WEDDING, I had all four of my wisdom teeth taken out at the dentist. Two weeks of sipping Sustagen through a straw had the weight falling off my already slight frame, and Iain's mum got busy taking in the wedding dress she had sewn for me.

My dress was simple. My dress was white.

For some brides, white stands for virginal purity. For me, it stood for Jesus washing me clean. My white dress represented forgiven-ness and the promise of a new life, and I felt the peace of that promise as, on our wedding day, Dad walked me down our church aisle towards Iain, who stood dressed in white at the front. Standing side by side, Iain and I pledged our love and lives to each other before God, family and friends. Col officiated, and at the end of an emotional ceremony he proudly pronounced us man and wife. After sharing a $2.50-a-head lunch in the college dining room with our guests, we headed off to honeymoon in a small shack belonging to a farming family in Kyogle. The ramshackle hut had no running water and a mattress so saggy we ended up dragging it onto the floor. But the property did have a trusting grey horse who came right up to the front door . . .

WHEN WE FIRST BEGAN working in ministry, I had no clue what a minister's wife should—or possibly more importantly, shouldn't—do. Was I supposed to wear dresses? Play the piano on Sundays? Lead the women's guild? I took my baffled thoughts to God, earnestly asking Him, "What do You expect of me as a minister's wife, Lord?" And He very clearly answered, "To be a wife and a mother, and to cherish

Me in your heart in everything you do." Immediately, every trace of pressure and inadequacy evaporated. Being a wife and mum was what I wanted to do, and knew I could do, with God's help. And cherishing Jesus in my heart seemed like the best calling in the world. And so it was that His three-fold job description became my true north.

Our wedding had marked the end of my year living at Bible College. I arrived there as a hard, dry sponge, but every day the lecturers and lectures were conduits of God's refreshing water, allowing me to soak in more and more without reaching saturation point. Every page I turned in the Bible held new treasures that set alight fires in my soul; they were life and health to me. I felt as though I had lived my whole life in a coma of ignorance and had now come alive for the first time. The curtain was drawn on the real world and, like a newborn baby with only hunger on its mind, I craved for more of the spiritual food that was changing me from the inside out. I went on to complete my diploma by correspondence, but I forever treasured that foundational year of my life as a newborn Christian.

CHAPTER NINE

I COULDN'T TASTE BLOOD—yet. My teeth sank hard into my bottom lip as I sat beside the twelve-year-old girl in the witness box.

How quickly perspectives can change . . .

Like the time I floated 1500 feet over Brisbane in a hot air balloon and, as we drifted heavenward, the people, cars and homes below shrank into little playing pieces on a boardgame. *Wow, Lord; up here I can see so many backyards, but down there, all I can see is my own. How small is my vision.*

Or the time when a fatherly fraud squad detective spoke less than twenty words, switching on a light in my eclipsed heart. Akin to a rescue worker coming upon a lost traveller, his words illuminated my path out of the dark hole I'd tumbled into.

Now it was my turn to shine light into other broken young lives. In the same police headquarters where I had once been interrogated and threatened with jail, I trained to be a volunteer PACT (Protect All Children Today) worker. My role involved preparing children, ranging in age from four to sixteen, to give evidence in criminal court proceedings. Apart from a few kids who were witnesses to a crime, most of the young people I supported were victims of crime themselves—typically sexual abuse. Once assigned a case, I'd visit the child in their home, or at a park if home was volatile. Developing rapport might mean shooting hoops or getting my fingernails painted—whatever they found interesting—in order to make a connection.

This was before cross-examination by closed-circuit television was mandated for child witnesses, and I took care to give them a personal tour of the legal system they were about to enter. We'd explore the empty courtroom, walking around together as I explained to the child where they would sit, what would be expected of them, and the roles and positions of the other people who would be present. On the day of the trial, I made sure we walked into the Magistrates Court side by side, and I'd sit close to the child as they were cross-examined. Reliving each minute detail of their abuse all over again was, in itself, an abusive experience for these children. Many defence lawyers mercilessly attacked the witnesses credibility, adding to the trauma as they tried to coerce the child into admitting that perhaps nothing had happened to them after all.

Our training had pulled no punches, and we were conditioned for two realities. One: this was not a justice system; it was a legal system in which the guilty often went free. Two: the evidence we'd be forced to hear would break even a hard heart. We were given various instructions on how to manage difficult hearings. *Pick a spot on the wall and focus on it intently. Bite your lip if you must. Whatever you do, don't lose control of your emotions.* Otherwise, we could instantly jeopardise a child's case. I figured I was an old hand at keeping my cool, well able to catch any emotions that dared raise their head and shove them back down to where they couldn't breathe or see the light of day. Even so, there were cases like this one, where I stared at a spot on the wall and bit my lip hard.

As I sat with the young girl waiting to be questioned, the man who had raped her was led into the dock. He was handcuffed, covered in tattoos, and he took a seat not far enough away from his victim who trembled beside me. My eyes bored into him, and I saw him growing uglier and uglier before me. *This man's heart is so dark it would leave a black smear on a piece of coal.* Anger and revenge rose so strongly in me that I felt them physically. The intensity of my thoughts shocked me. I wanted to see this man hurting— and hurting badly—for what he had done. If he was a fly, I would have ripped his wings off, hoping it hurt like hell. Then I would have smashed him over and over with the biggest sledgehammer I could swing.

Suddenly and unmistakably, amid my roiling emotions, I sensed the Lord's hand on my shoulder. He was speaking to me: "I love this man, as much as I love you." *God . . . how could you even **think** of us in the same thought? Look at what he has done!* "I hate his sin more than you will ever be able to hate it. But I died for him, just as I died for you." In seconds, the hatred within me dissipated. It was just and right to want him to be punished for his crimes, but not once had it crossed my mind that Jesus loved him. He loved this outcast. No matter who he was, what he'd done, or how grotesque he appeared, Jesus looked at him with a love that pierced beyond the ugliness. Everything that man needed to be clean and righteous was offered to him freely by Jesus Christ—the same way it had been offered to me.

Even as my heart broke in two for this child whose innocence had been stripped away, and who would likely endure her own life sentence because of what this man had done to her, I repented of my boiling hatred against the criminal before me.

For abuse victims, the most traumatising outcome is to hear the gavel come down and the judge announce, "Not guilty." Then their perpetrator smiles and walks away, free, while bars lock around the child's own heart, sealing them in a prison of pain and fear. This young person then lives with the knowledge that no one believes them; no one is taking their side. Sometimes, in a twist that was always hardest for me to comprehend, not even their mother would stand beside them. Mercifully, in the rape case of the young girl I was supporting, the man for whom Christ died received a jail sentence.

In the seven years I worked with PACT, too many times I watched a young person's shoulders slump heavily as their hope for justice was lost. As we left the courtroom together, I would listen with an aching heart as they hinted at finding a way to end their pain. I prayed for words to give them— words to shine a light towards a more hopeful future, one in which they might gather up the courage they needed to keep on living. And I prayed that, just as He had done for me, God would show them there was more to their story than this seemingly crushing end.

IF ONLY JAMIE HAD known that.

What goes through a person's brain just before a bullet enters it?

In deep waters with drug dealers and seeing no way out, Jamie put a gun in his mouth and pulled the trigger, leaving his wife and two children with a soul-destroying legacy and loss.

Finding out about Jamie's death was like having a dirty knife cut me to the soul. A river of grief washed over me at the heart-wrenching reality that Jamie's eternity was likely one without God. Satan had had a plan for Jamie's life, just as surely as God did. But the thief had come. He had stolen. He had killed. I was so angry at the enemy for what he had destroyed.

My own healing journey took time. It was as though God took it gently, not wanting to break me any more than I already was. Even so, He exposed my hidden pain bit by bit, while over and over I thought, *I'm healed, set free, forgiven, washed clean, the fear is gone . . .* only to find that the ghost of the past cast a long shadow. A shampoo scent, the same colour car, the boss' name on someone else, the beach, a particular song, even a sermon—so many triggers unearthed gut-punching pain, pain I wasn't even aware lay buried within until it reared in full force, choking my heart. But the deepest fear I walked with daily was a simple one: *What if I see my old boss again?* I had no capacity; no strategy for what to do if I came face to face with the man himself.

As the Lord carried me through healing, gently putting the fragments of my life back together, I absorbed the truth that He had experienced incomparable abuse, torture and pain. Jesus' tears mingled with mine as slowly but surely I moved further away from pain and closer to peace. I never saw the boss again, but it would take seven years before my fear finally ran out of oxygen.

CHAPTER TEN

"As natural as being a woman!"

The ad for sanitary napkins blared from the TV, reminding me that not menstruating made me only half a woman. As if I could forget. Many young women I knew cursed their monthly cycles due to the disruption or pain it brought them. But the loss of this regular affliction in my life made me feel defective; less than whole. The advert's cheery voice carried on in the background, unaware that the sharp jab had sunk its teeth into me. *That's all I am . . . half.* Before Iain and I married, I visited a medical specialist to seek help for my infertility. He prescribed a hormone treatment with the aim of causing a 'breakthrough' bleed to prime the pump for a menstrual cycle. That didn't happen. What did happen was that the drugs darkened my mood, planting black thoughts of jumping off the Story Bridge, cigarette in hand. Finally, the gynaecologist drove the prognosis home: "You are infertile. There is no hope of you having children. If you want a family, I suggest you put in for adoption as soon as you can." That was that, then. I couldn't be helped by human hands, and there was a two-year waiting period following marriage before we could even apply for adoption.

Once we were married, Col had prayed fervently over Iain and me for the blessing of children. I also released my desire to God, praying, "Father, if You choose to give us children, we will trust You. If not, as disappointed as we will be, we will trust You." I had meant every word, but six months into married life, the knowledge that I was less than whole was breaking me into little pieces.

One evening, while Iain was at university, I slumped at the kitchen table and surrendered my tears to the tablecloth. The radio played softly in the background as I let months of longing, shame and self-pity spill out in deep, private sobs. Suddenly, as though a hand was fine-tuning the radio, the words of a song reached me distinctly: "You're once, twice, three times a lady, and I love you." In that moment, Jesus took those words and sang them into my spirit. He wanted me to know that, even though my body wasn't functioning properly, I was a whole woman. In His eyes I was complete. I don't know the rest of the song—I didn't even hear it. God had beautifully validated my worth in His eyes, and the flood of grief became a torrent of wonder and happiness right there at the kitchen table.

The next morning, I woke to a shock discovery—a not-so-familiar red stain on my undies. My breath caught in my throat, and a deep understanding sank into my soul. Last night, listening to a song I had never heard before, God had not only restored my sense of worth—He had also healed my broken body. That welcome red tinge was the beginning of my first period in over two years. What a miracle! All I could give Him in response to His love was a humble and grateful heart.

For three months, the miracle of womanhood continued. Then, just as suddenly as it had started, it stopped. A queasy sensation hovered in the background, and my breasts felt strange. *Could it be?* I made a doctor's appointment, waiting nervously for the blood test results. At the follow-up appointment, as I sat in his office, my stomach churning, the doctor looked down at his paperwork, looked up at me, and gave a wondrous announcement: "You're pregnant." Unlike the last time I'd been given that pronouncement incorrectly, this time I eagerly believed it!

I walked home from the clinic in stunned amazement. My whole world had just flipped upside down. I felt as though I had been transported into a wondrous world where all of life's issues paled into insignificance in the face of the realisation that a new life was growing inside my womb. Suddenly, miraculously, I was carrying another human being! Our very own baby.

The pregnancy went well—the birth, not so much. But as the Bible aptly puts it: "A woman giving birth to a child has pain because her time has come; but when her baby is born she forgets the anguish because of her joy that a child is born into the world" (John 16:21). Our son—our miracle—was born into the world, filling our hearts with bucket loads of joy.

One year passed, then another, but my periods didn't return. Once again, it appeared I was barren. I was learning that stressing and fretting about it achieved nothing, except perhaps some unwelcome frown lines. Instead, turning to the source of our first-born joy, we asked our heavenly Father to give us another child. And again, miraculously, my monthly cycle started. After four cycles, I fell pregnant with our second miracle. After our beautiful daughter was weaned, my periods returned regularly and soon we were blessed with our third miracle and second precious daughter.

In the midst of our rejoicing, one Bible verse in particular became my testimony: "God raises the poor from the dust and lifts the needy from the ash heap; He seats them with princes, with the princes of their people. He settles the barren woman in her home, as a happy mother of children. Praise the Lord" (Psalm 113:7-9).

EPILOGUE

"YOU HAVE THE HEART of a lion, my friend."

With love and admiration in the palm of my hand, I patted my spirited palomino mare. There's nowhere she wouldn't go when I asked her—up mountains, into blind lantana-filled scrubs and gullies, across flooded creeks, or around the edges of steep, rocky hillsides. Unshod and sure-footed, she gave her all whenever we mustered wild scrub cattle in untamed bushland. Deep trust linked us together . . .

How clear a picture of the trust I am growing in you, Father. The more I know you, the freer I am to run . . .

And the chase was on! Thundering along the creek bank in hot pursuit, my mount and I strained to turn the scrub bull and drive it back towards the yards. As we bolted over grassy hills and dips, ducking low-hanging tree branches, all of a sudden the feral bull went from full bolt to a dead stop. We pulled up alongside it, hooves stuttering in the dirt, and for a split second my mind went blank with bewilderment.

Blowing heavily through flared nostrils, the maddened animal turned, lowered its head and lunged, trying to stab its sharp horns into my horse's belly. And just like that, we were the hunted. Instinctively, my mare spun in a tight circle and we bolted, galloping back the way we had come until the wild bull lost interest and disappeared over the creek bank.

Every muster in that untamed country gave our team exciting adventures, some of which involved a whisker's width between us and injury. I wholeheartedly agree with the bull rider who said, "Sometimes I look back on my life and am seriously impressed I'm still alive!"

Father, how many times have You saved me from fire and flood and bull's horns and lion's dens and spat me out of big fish mouths? How could I ever count the good and perfect gifts You have given me?

For a baker's dozen years, I relished my work mustering cattle on horseback just west of Imbil. It impacted me deeply that God had brought me full circle—I was back in the place where I had retreated for safety long years before.

One typically hot day, I carried a chair down to the creek where we pushed the cattle through to reach the yards. Seating myself at the water's edge, I quietly asked Jesus what was on His mind for me next. As I lazily ran my gaze across nature's humble beauty, I found myself staring at the deep ruts on the other side of the creek. Two grooves ran from the bank right down to the water, forming the tracks we pushed the cattle down; tracks they followed to come and drink. As I observed the two routes that had been carved by so many hooves, I pondered on the paths that make up life—and I shared my thoughts with Jesus.

"Lord, the choices I've made have led me along a track. Maybe like that right-hand track. But if I'd taken the left-hand route, would I have made better choices? Cherished You more and borne more fruit? Been a better wife and mum?"

And then, in the stillness of the summer morning, I sensed His answer:

"It wouldn't matter which track you had taken. If you'd chosen the left path, some things would have been better, but challenges would still arise. They'd just be different challenges. But My grace would have been sufficient for you on that other track too. I still would have used those challenges to gently make you more like Me."

I leaned back in my chair, a soft smile of gratitude settling on my face. The persistent hound dog of regret had once again come up against Jesus' faithfulness, and lost. My Saviour's peace which surpasses human understanding, settled my disquieted heart.

SINCE WELCOMING HIM AS a travel companion, my wagon ride with Jesus hasn't always been one I'd proudly hang my hat on. At times, my heart has gone as rogue as a scrub bull. I've grieved over failures and lived with regrets. But I've also learned that trying to be perfect is like trying to put a yoke on a feral bull. Aside from the insanity of even attempting it, such an undertaking just wouldn't work. Nor would it be the 'easy yoke' that Jesus promised His followers. I know now that I am what I am, by the grace of God. And as the years stack on, that grace gives me more and more to be grateful for, and more and more to look forward to.

I now straddle two worlds—this one, where I serve

Jesus and seek to love my family with a 'love that always protects' (1 Corinthians 13); and the one that is waiting for me—a world of endless joy where I'll gallop alongside Jesus forever.

ACKNOWLEDGEMENTS

Father God . . . Your grace has rewritten my story, You haven't finished writing yet, and You'll never give up on me. This human pen falters trying to find a deep enough, 'Thank You'.

Iain . . . I haven't met anyone who dishes out more genuine grace than you. Life hasn't been all shade and downhill, but God sure has taken us on a great ride together.

My children . . . You are precious gifts—loved beyond measure, our prayed-for miracles. More than anything else in this world, I want to see you in the next.

My grandchildren and beyond . . . Here is the story of one of your grandparents (I wish I could tell you more about mine, but I've only met one and her memory is faded). If my prayers are answered, you too will come to know God's amazing grace in your lives.

Mum and Dad . . . Becoming a parent made me realise how deep and wide your love has always been. Any shortcomings (I have a ton) are completely overshadowed by the ways you have loved long and given endlessly. Thank you.

Jeff and Jenny . . . Thank you for leading me to Jesus, for loving and discipling me, and for being instrumental in me going to Bible College.

My mentors and mates . . . There's a saying that the woman who heals herself, heals her children. I didn't heal myself—God did, and many of you were a part of His rebuild in my life, teaching me godly wisdom and riding alongside me in my spiritual journey.

To the Salvation Army Officer's daughter . . . I tried to find you to let you know the truth wasn't wasted on me. Thank you for sharing the gospel. I'm a believer now, and I'll see you in heaven.

To the Fraud Squad detective . . . I tried to find you too. Thanks for being fatherly enough to shoot an arrow of truth into my desperate heart, changing the trajectory of my life.

To connect with Linda Watt, please email her at:
aussiechristiancowgirl@gmail.com

Also by Linda Watt

God's signature is all over the Aussie bush. Here, in 52 rural devotions, you'll discover seasoned drovers, cattle herds, stock horses, working dogs, swagmen, rodeo riders, cattle duffers, timber fellers, fences and floods. God is the God of the outback, and the bush offers lessons richer than any classroom! Roll out your swag, boil the billy, pull up a log, and enjoy the abundance of life and faith in the bush.

Available from Amazon.

www.ingramcontent.com/pod-product-compliance
Lightning Source LLC
Chambersburg PA
CBHW030221140626
46545CB00011B/803